KV-602-932

1

2

3

WITHDRAWN
FROM
UNIVERSITY OF PLYMOUTH

90 0559708 1

From Key Stage 2 to Key Stage 3: Smoothing the Transfer for Pupils with Learning Difficulties

by
Dorothy Smith

A NASEN Publication

Published in 2000

© Dorothy Smith

All rights reserved. No part of this publication may be reproduced or transmitted in any form or by any means, electronic, mechanical, photocopying, recording, or otherwise without the prior permission of the publishers.

ISBN 1 901485 25 0

The right of Dorothy Smith to be identified as author of this work has been asserted by her in accordance with the Copyright, Designs and Patents Act 1988.

Published by NASEN.
NASEN is a registered charity. Charity No. 1007023.
NASEN is a company limited by guarantee, registered in England and Wales. Company No. 2674379.

Further copies of this book and details of NASEN's many other publications may be obtained from NASEN Bookshop at its registered office:
NASEN House, 4/5, Amber Business Village, Amber Close, Amington, Tamworth, Staffs. B77 4RP.
Tel: 01827 311500; Fax: 01827 313005
Email: welcome@nasen.org.uk; Web site: www.nasen.org.uk

Copy editing by Nicola von Schrieber.
Cover design by Raphael Creative Design.
Typeset by J. C. Typesetting.
Typeset in Times and printed in the United Kingdom by Stowes (Stoke-on-Trent).